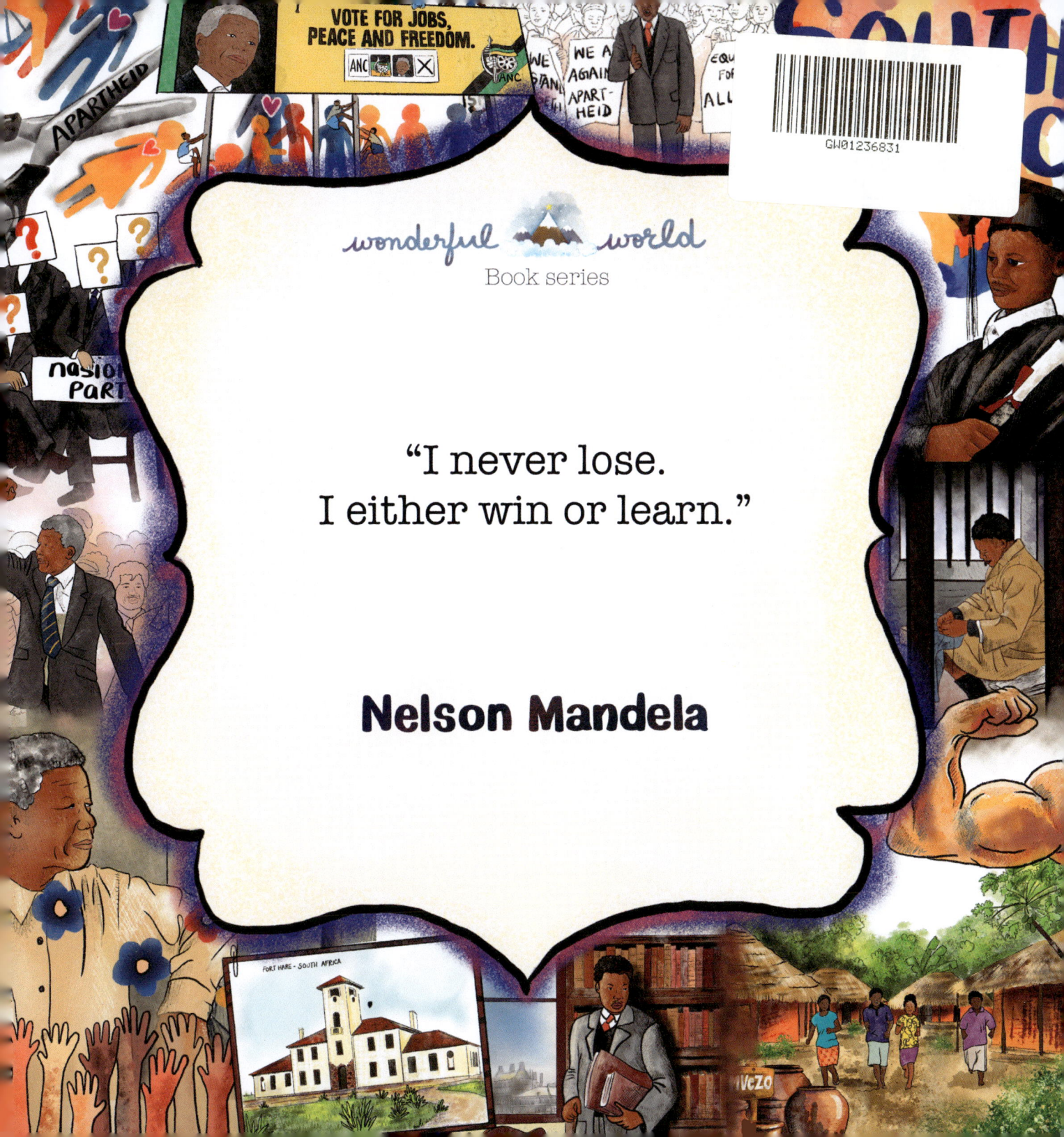

wonderful world
Book series

"I never lose.
I either win or learn."

Nelson Mandela

In a world of different colours like **yellow**, **red**, and **blue**,

Everything's a rainbow—
flowers, fruit, and people too.

Some might look like you,
and some might not,

Though we're all the same inside, no matter what.

But in **South Africa**,
not so long ago,

A few people were very **ignorant**, so

Ignorant: Not knowing many things.

They made a cruel system called the **Apartheid**

Cruel: Being very mean.

Which was a set of rules meant to divide,

So people of different colours couldn't mix or meet

Or marry or be friends or sit together and eat.

Obscene: Disgusting / Rude.

Nelson Rolihlala Mandela
knew this wasn't right,

And this is the story of how
he put up a fight.

Mandela was born in **Mvezo,** a tiny village,
(Muh-vay-z-oh)

And was the first in his family to go to college.

While studying in the University of Fort Hare,

He saw the effects of the Apartheid everywhere.

Then he went to Johannesburg to study **law,**

Law: Rules which everyone in a country has to follow.

Where he protested against the **injustices** he saw.

Injustice: When something is not fair.

He was imprisoned for twenty seven years,

Imprisoned: Being kept in prison. A prison is a place where people are kept as punishment.

But he **stayed strong** despite all his fears.

He was chosen as the leader
when he was set free,

Mandela also won the **Nobel Prize for Peace,**

because he stayed true to all his **beliefs.**

Beliefs: The thought that something is true.

So if something's wrong or bothers you,
please speak up!

You can talk to a friend
or a trusted grown-up.

You have the **power**
to set everything right.

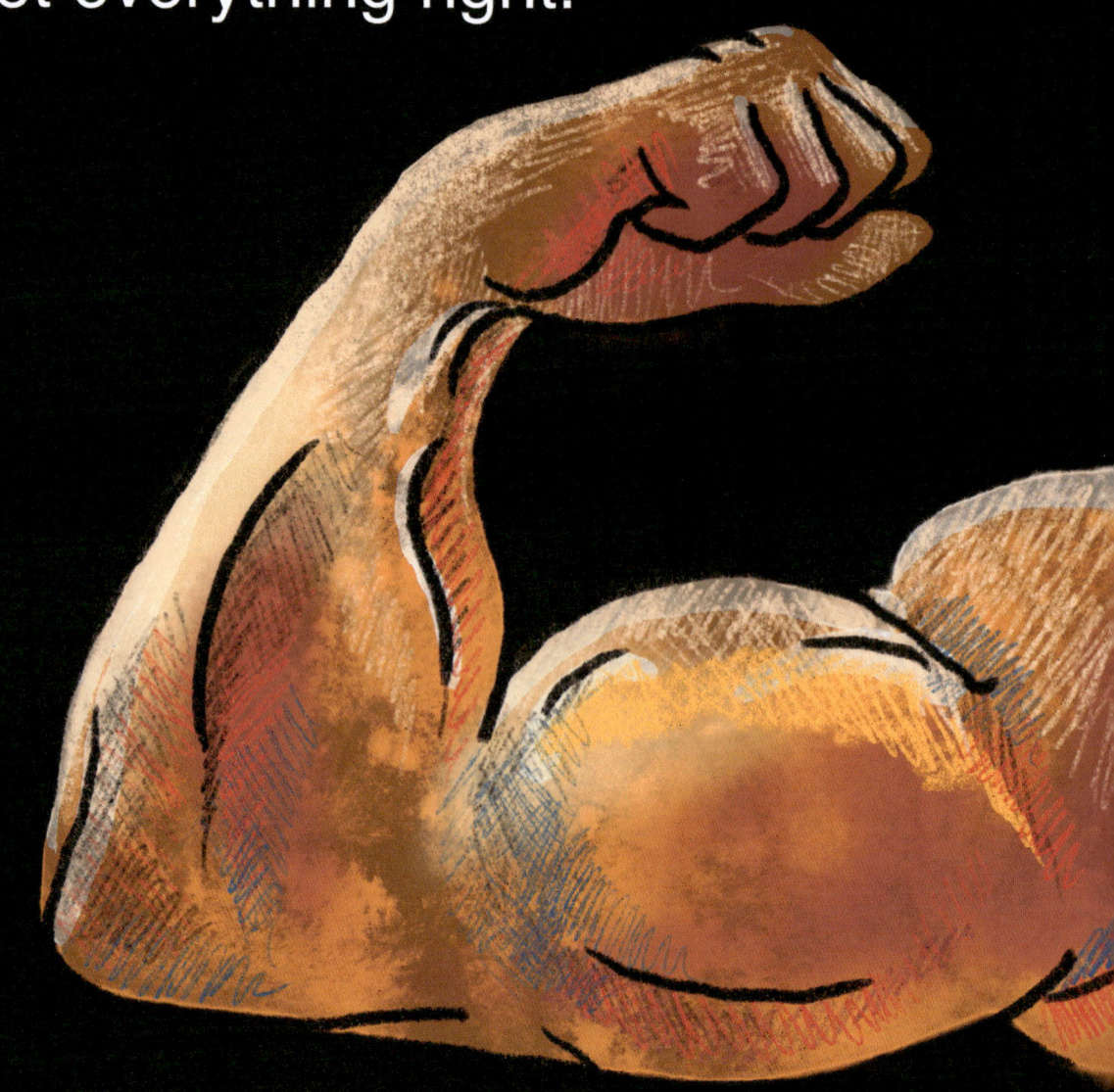

Even the smallest flame lights up the darkest night.

Mandela was **brave,**
and an **inspiring leader** too,

A wonderful person—
just like you!

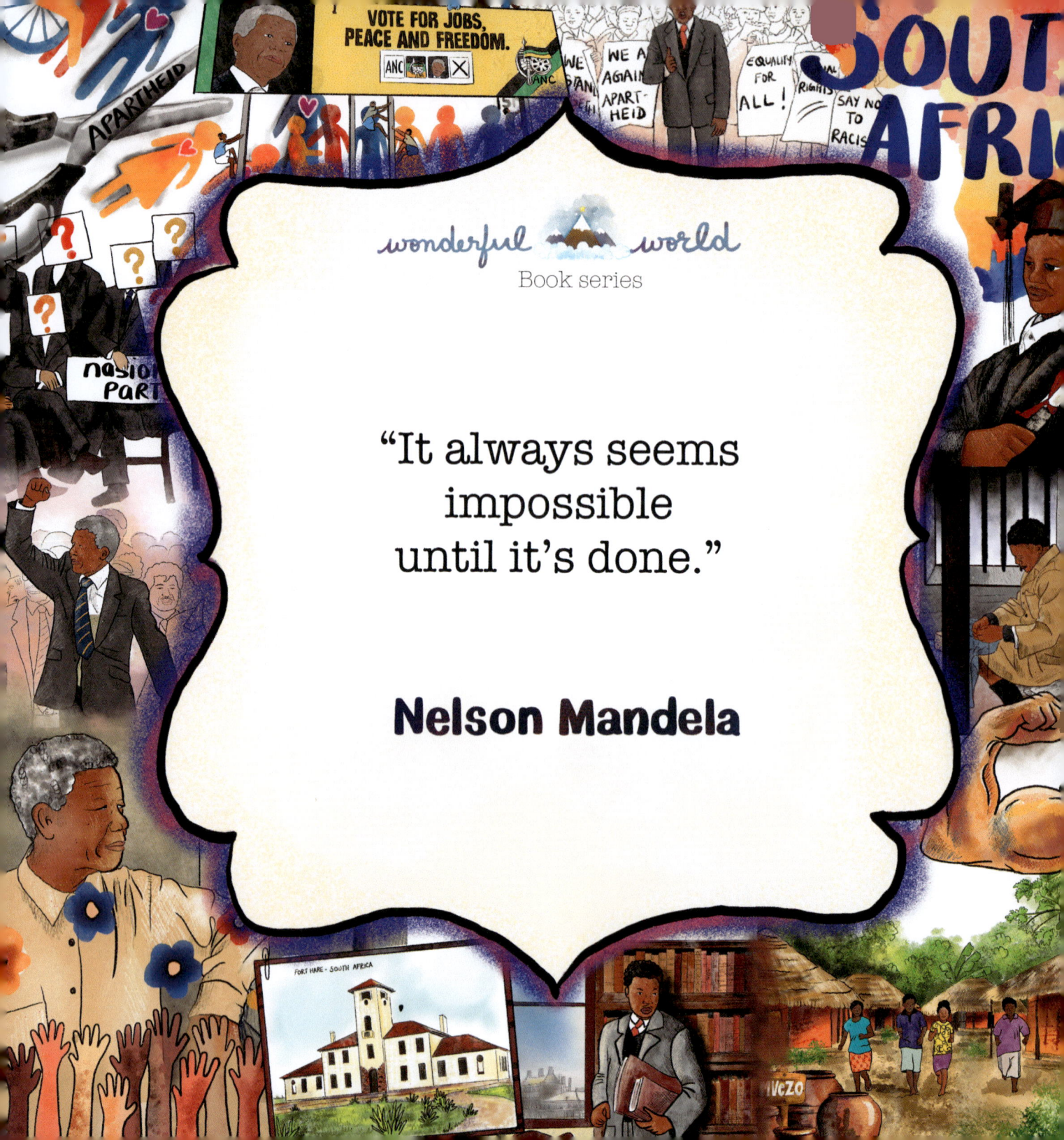

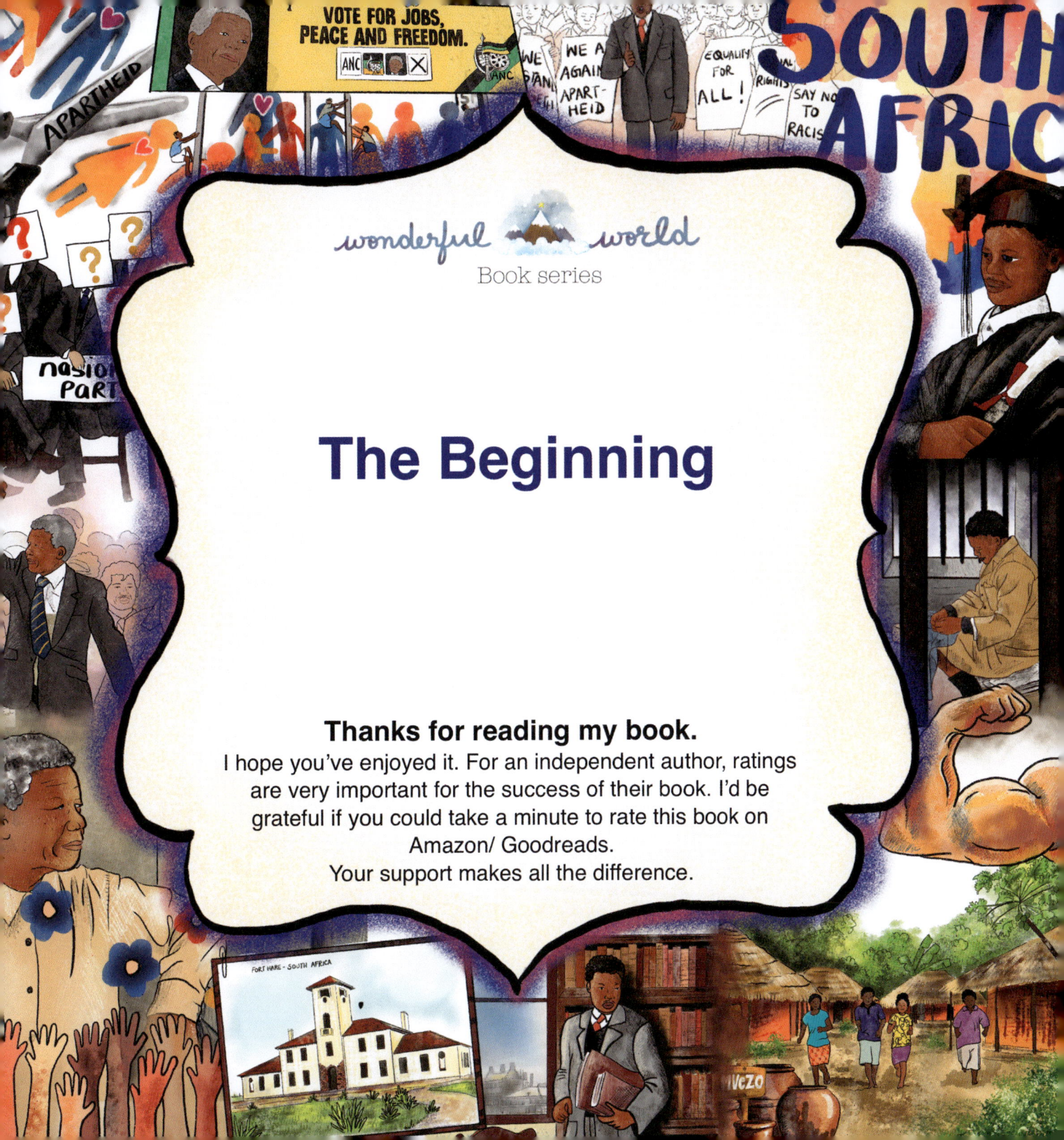

wonderful world
Book series

The Beginning

Thanks for reading my book.
I hope you've enjoyed it. For an independent author, ratings are very important for the success of their book. I'd be grateful if you could take a minute to rate this book on Amazon/ Goodreads.
Your support makes all the difference.

Glossary

Ignorant: Not knowing many things.

Cruel: Being very mean.

Obscene: Disgusting / Rude.

Law: Rules which everyone in a country has to follow.

Injustice: When something is not fair.

Imprisoned: Being kept in prison.
A prison is a place where people are kept as punishment.

Beliefs: The thought that something is true.

Freedom: The right to act, speak, think as you would want to, and the right to live peacefully and happily.

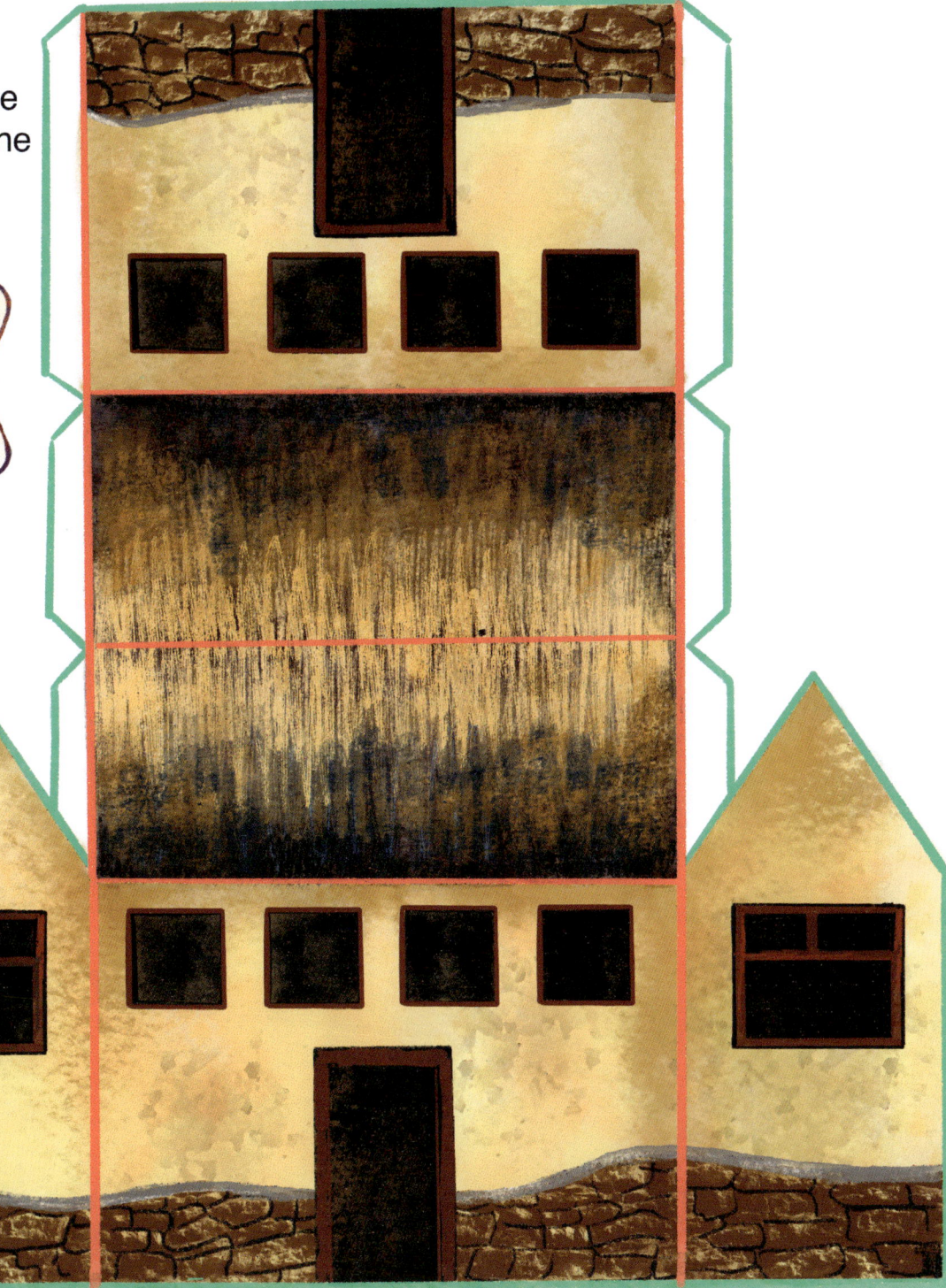

A simplified house of the kind seen in Mvezo.

Spot the Difference

Can you find six differences between the two pictures?

Answers (but how much do differences matter really?) In the second picture, 1. The banana tree at the back is missing. 2. The girl in the middle has a different coloured skirt. 3. The shirt hanging is a different colour. 4. The spelling of Mvezo is wrong. 5. There is a ball. 6. The bush in front has flowers

wonderful world
Book series

About the Author

Author, illustrator, and dentist, **Ramya Julian** finished her first novel at the age of ten and she avers it was very well received though it was read only by her brother.

She has all the hobbies of a maiden Victorian aunt – reading, writing, painting, crocheting, knitting and sewing, and the temperament of one. When she's not guilt-tripping her two daughters into good behaviour, she can be found devouring books, crafting poems and puns, and chuckling at her own witticisms. She grew up in India and now lives with her husband and their two daughters in London.

She has experienced so much joy through the enchanting artistry of many authors and creators, that she aspires to share at least some of it through her writing.

To see more of her work, visit **www.ramyajulian.com**

www.ramyajulian.com

Also in this series

NEXT IN LINE: MANY MANY MORE WONDERFUL DIVERSE HEROES

TO MY NEWSLETTER
For the latest news and free printables
www.ramyajulian.com

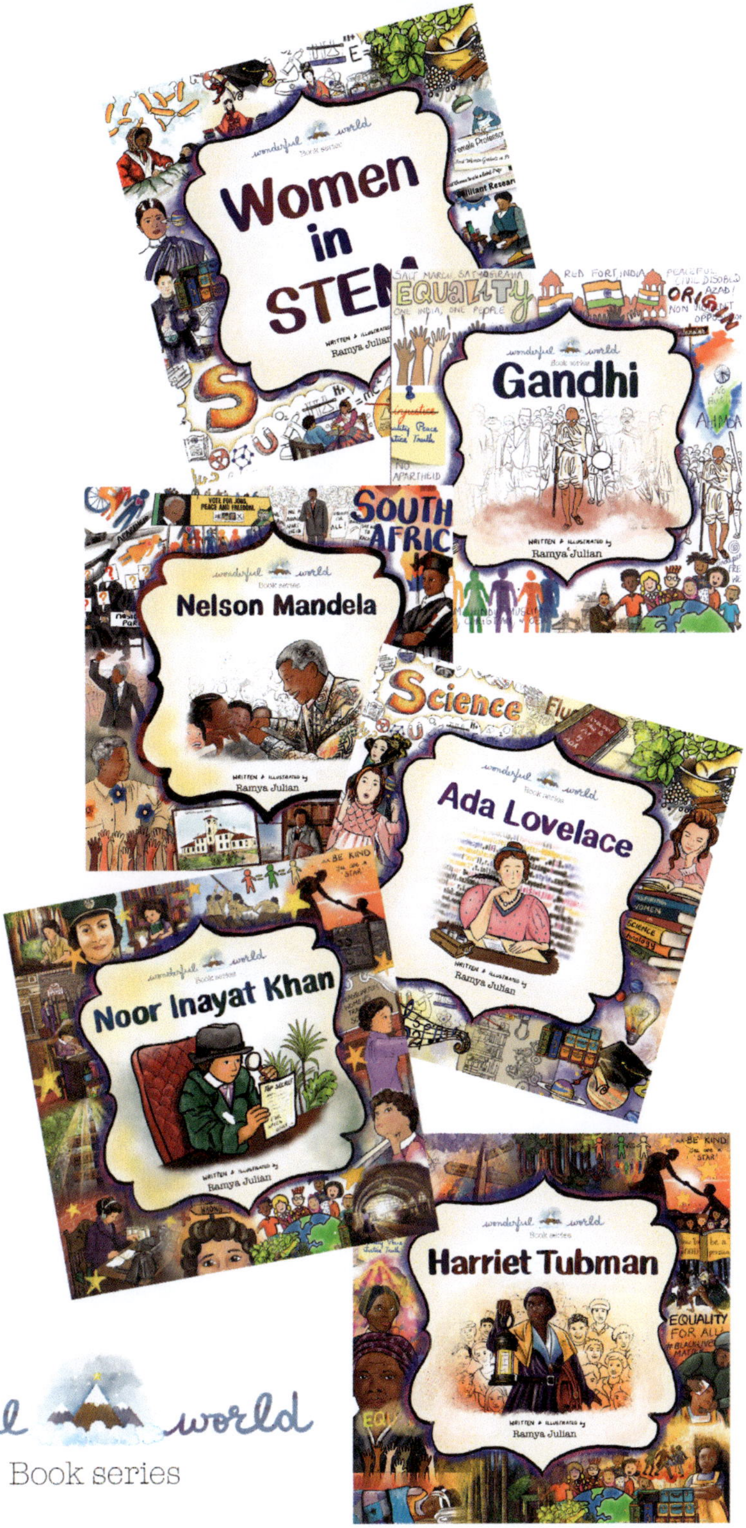

@RAMYAJULIAN

wonderful world
Book series

Printed in Great Britain
by Amazon